THE LITTLE BOOK OF

WATCHES

First published in Great Britain in 2026 by Cassell,
an imprint of
Octopus Publishing Group Ltd
Carmelite House
50 Victoria Embankment
London EC4Y 0DZ
www.octopusbooks.co.uk

An Hachette UK Company
www.hachette.co.uk

The authorized representative in the EEA is
Hachette Ireland
8 Castlecourt Centre, Dublin 15, D15 XTP3
email: info@hbgi.ie

Distributed in the US by Hachette Book Group
1290 Avenue of the Americas, 4th and 5th Floors
New York, NY 10104

Distributed in Canada by Canadian Manda Group
664 Annette St., Toronto, Ontario, Canada
M6S 2C8

This book was conceived, designed, and
produced by The Bright Press, an imprint of the
Quarto Group,
1 Triptych Place, 185 Park Street,
London, United Kingdom, SE1 9SH
T (0)2077 009 000
www.Quarto.com

Publisher: James Evans
Editorial Director: Isheeta Mustafi
Managing Editor: Lucy Tipton
Art Director: Emily Nazer
Senior Editor: Nick Pierce
Project Editor: Anna Southgate
Designer: Wayne Blades
Picture Researcher: Charlotte Rivers
Illustrations: Sarah Skeate

ISBN: 978-1-78840-698-7
eISBN: 978-1-78840-711-3

A CIP catalogue record for this book is available from the British Library.

Printed and bound in Guangdong, China.

TT/06/26

10 9 8 7 6 5 4 3 2 1

MIX
Paper | Supporting responsible forestry
FSC® C016973
FSC
www.fsc.org

This FSC® label means that materials used for the product have been responsibly sourced.

THE LITTLE BOOK OF
WATCHES

LEGENDARY BRANDS AND THE
WATCHES THAT DEFINED THEM

JOSHUA SIMS

CONTENTS

INTRODUCTION

For those who wear them, mechanical watches tend to evoke a passionate interest that can leave the uninitiated perplexed. After all, isn't a mechanical watch outmoded in the digital age? The same can be said for record players, film cameras and other analogue technologies that elicit a similar fanaticism. There will be an element of nostalgia, of course, and a level of human-friendly interaction that digital alternatives cannot replicate – a certain sound, a look, a way of operating the device. In the case of mechanical watches, the appeal is precisely because they're mechanical.

Of course, a smartwatch can do so much more, as can a cheap digital watch, available now for more than half a century. What these cannot do, however, is tell the time with the remarkable reliability and precision that can be achieved using an assembly of hundreds of cogs, wheels, springs and levers small enough to fit into a neat unit that will sit comfortably on your wrist – all dust-, water- and shock-free.

Dial up that micro-engineering, which has kept improving for over a century, and such a watch might have any range of additional features that include the ability to record elapsed time, to show

12
OMEGA
PROFESSIONAL

the day, date and month (accounting for varying lengths of months and even the occasional leap year), to display the phases of the moon and to chime the time on demand. A very impressive mechanical watch can do all of these things, *and* without the use of any circuitry, chips or batteries. What's more, as the esteemed British watchmaker Roger Smith once noted: if looked after, said watch will be able to do these things forever – long after digital tech has been outmoded. A century or five hence, an engineer will be able to open up a mechanical watch and understand exactly how it works and, if necessary, how to make it work again.

Naturally, there is more to consider than mechanics: there's appreciation for a watch as a design object, as a piece of jewellery, as a status symbol. But these are bonuses. The mechanical watch remains because of how it works, not just what it might say.

PAGE 7: Omega Seamaster.
OPPOSITE: (Top) The intricate detail of a watch mechanism; (bottom) Audemars Piguet Royal Oak.

A BRIEF HISTORY OF THE WRISTWATCH

FROM POCKET TO WRIST

Given the long history of watches, the idea of wearing one on the wrist is relatively new. Carrying a form of time-telling device about the person dates back to the 16th century, when German clockmaker Peter Henlein is attributed with devising what was effectively a small, primitive, key-wound clock in a brass box to be worn on a chain around the neck.

Over time, and to make them more comfortable, these pendant watches were smoothed into more of a pebble shape and became known as 'Nuremberg eggs'. Yet it was only with a change of fashion – specifically the advent of the waistcoat, popularized by England's King Charles II from 1666 – that carrying a watch in a pocket, attached to one's clothing by chain or fob, encouraged the development of flatter, smaller watches, essentially the first pocket watches.

Decorative as well as utilitarian, early pocket watches blurred the line between jewellery and timepiece, being heavily gem-set and engraved. Certainly, they were considered luxury items for the very well-off and gentlemanly. Only with the standardization of watch parts and other practical advances, such as the invention of winding by use of

PONCTUA
PONCTUA
LA MEILLEURE MONTRE DE PRÉCISION LA MOINS CHÈRE
PUBLICITÉ WALL, 16, Rue Lafayette, PARIS.

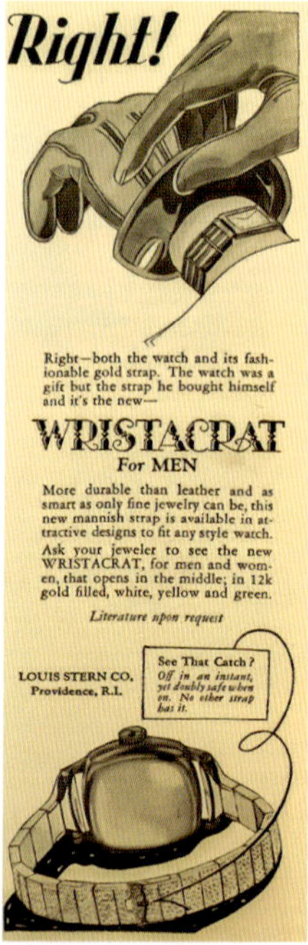
Right!
Right—both the watch and its fashionable gold strap. The watch was a gift but the strap he bought himself and it's the new—
WRISTACRAT
For MEN
More durable than leather and as smart as only fine jewelry can be, this new mannish strap is available in attractive designs to fit any style watch.
Ask your jeweler to see the new WRISTACRAT, for men and women, that opens in the middle; in 12k gold filled, white, yellow and green.
Literature upon request
LOUIS STERN CO.
Providence, R.I.
See That Catch? Off in an instant, yet doubly safe when on. No other strap has it.

a crown in the 1800s, did pocket watches become more widely accessible. With major social developments, such as the expansion of the railways and the growth of factory employment, came a growing need to know the time, and life for many became increasingly shaped by clocks and watches.

The first watches worn on the wrist were a product of fashion, too: Queen Elizabeth I's favourite, Robert Dudley, is believed to have commissioned a bejewelled 'bracelet watch' for her, and aristocratic women took to wearing such items widely from the early 1800s. The first wristwatch designed for time-telling and not ornament was likely made in France by the great watchmaker Abraham-Louis Breguet for Queen Maria Carolina of Naples in 1810, with Patek Philippe making the first Swiss wristwatch, in 1868, for a countess. It would be another century – and a more obvious practical necessity – before men made the move from carrying a watch in the pocket to wearing one on the wrist.

PAGE 10: Sean Connery, in the 1979 American adventure thriller *Cuba*.
PREVIOUS PAGE: French opera singer Pedro Gailhard wears a pocket watch, c.1880.
OPPOSITE: (Top left) French advert for a Ponctua pocket watch, 1906.
(top right) 1920s advertisement; (bottom) vintage wristwatches.

FLYERS AND FIGHTERS

The breakthrough moment came when the trailblazing Brazilian aviator Alberto Santos-Dumont realized that it was frustratingly hard to operate both his aircraft and – since timekeeping was critical to the flying competitions of the early 20th century – his pocket watch. Fortunately, his friend Louis Cartier suggested a solution: a square-cased watch mounted on a leather strap. Santos-Dumont went on to set the world speed record in 1906 and was the first person to be photographed in flight — all good publicity.

That men found the wristwatch more practical slowly signalled the end of the pocket watch, with World War I (1914–18) proving to be the tipping point. As with flying, there was a rapid recognition that keeping both hands free in battle was a good idea. A 1916 British Army equipment handbook lists the wristwatch (along with binoculars and a pistol) as essential equipment for officers.

Cartier's wristwatch was still highly decorated, yet wartime watches encouraged the development of more robust, everyday models: the first attempts at shock resistance and luminescence, for example, arose from the needs of watches used in action.

ABOVE: This magazine advert for Cartier's Tank alludes to the creation of the Santos-Dumont watch.

PILOT'S WATCH

Accurate timekeeping was essential when navigating an aircraft using early compass transmitters. Watches allowed pilots to calculate their position relative to north according to the number of seconds that followed a full minute from picking up the signal. For the process to work, synchronicity with a reference clock was essential.

Though Cartier had made a wristwatch for Brazilian aviator Alberto Santos-Dumont, it was not until 1931 that a manufacturer considered meeting the pilot's needs more precisely, and only then because American aviator Charles Lindbergh's watch failed during his record-breaking transatlantic flight. Lindbergh persuaded Longines to create the Hour Angle watch to his specifications. A nonslip, outsized bezel with a zero mark allowed easier timing of compass transmitter signals, and an outsized crown allowed it to be operated while wearing gloves. Later developments led to antimagnetic and chronograph watches.

The defining characteristics of the design gave the pilot's watch a certain machismo: a larger dial for maximum legibility, typically white on black, with luminous hands and an ability to perform in tough conditions. In the early days, flying involved strong vibrations and outside temperatures of –44°C (–47°F).

Soft, iron-core case
Sub-dials
Bezel
Slide-rule indicators
Date display

THE RISE OF THE SWISS

Apple (at the time of writing) may make more watches every year than the entire output of the watch industry in Switzerland. Swiss watchmaking may account for a tiny part of the country's national GDP, and just five of Switzerland's 350 or so watch brands may account for around half of all Swiss watch sales. Yet Swiss watchmaking dominates in impact and in reputation, and this despite the fact that many other countries once had strong watch industries of their own.

How did Switzerland come to be the watchmaking superpower? History plays a part. Going back to 1491, in France, Catholics were busy forcibly displacing the Protestant population, which just happened to include most of the world-class watchmakers of the era. Some went to England, the Netherlands or Scandinavia, but most went to Switzerland, just a hop across the border.

Swiss culture has played a role, too. Historically a poor, farming nation, long, hard winters left people seeking seasonal employment that could be done anywhere without the need for the kind of major industrial infrastructure typically found around big cities: watch assembly was one solution.

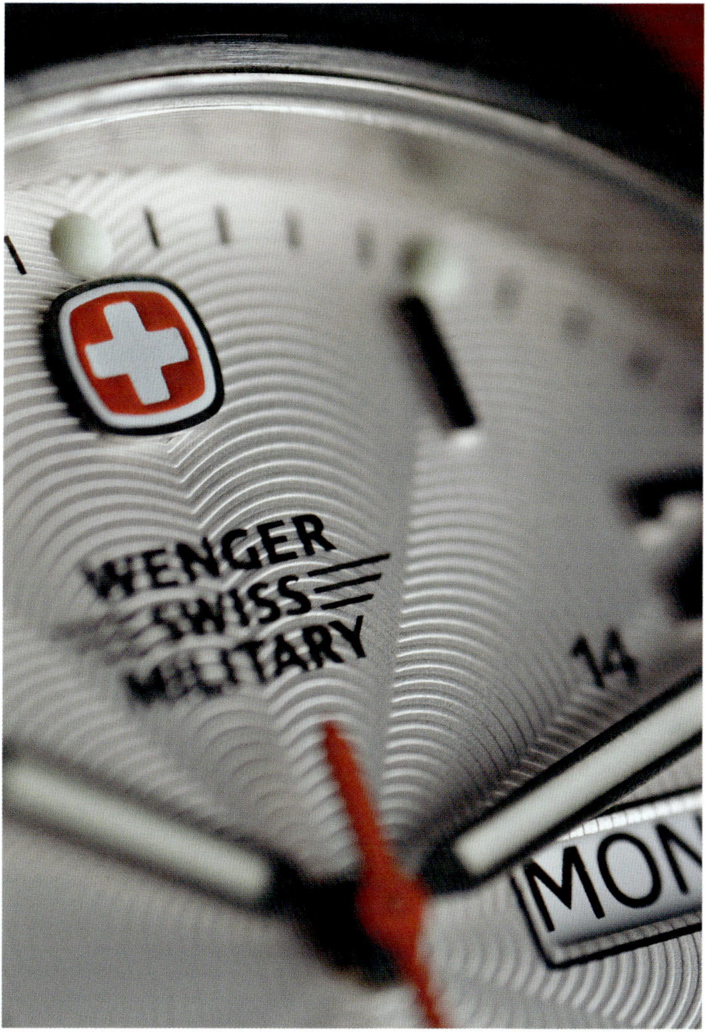
WENGER
SWISS
MILITARY
14
MON

UNIVERSAL
GENEVE

Then there was politics. In 1541 the city of Geneva, experiencing religious upheaval with the imposition of Calvinist austerity, actually banned gold jewellery. Craftspeople turned instead to making watches, developing an early expertise in the process. Consider geo-politics, too: World Wars I and II did much to kill off what was left of many nations' watchmaking industries, either through occupation or through a necessary shift to making military equipment and instrumentation for the war effort. Being neutral, Switzerland found itself with an effective monopoly, and free to continue to develop its civilian offer.

Add in a concerted and consistent global marketing effort and it is small surprise that, when it comes to watches, 'Made in Switzerland' carries the same cachet as 'Made in France' does for wine and 'Made in Germany' for cars.

PAGE 21: A Swiss flag replaces the numeral 12 on a Wenger Swiss military watch.
OPPOSITE: (Top) 1940s Universal Genève Calatrava; (bottom) vintage Swiss watches.

FIELD WATCH

The field watch has its origins in World War I, when accurate timings for assaults or artillery bombardments became increasingly important to military success. During World War II, a number of Swiss-made field watches were made for the British Army by the likes of Longines and Omega, and lesser-known brands such as Vertex and super-rare Grana. With 12 models in total, these desirable pieces are called The Dirty Dozen, after the 1967 war film.

Intended for use by soldiers, the watches follow military specifications and are all remarkably similar. The design demanded a small case, bold Arabic numerals on a black background with a minute track, luminosity, shatterproof glass, a second hand, and a hacking movement, which stops the second hand when the crown is pulled out in order to make synchronization more precise. These so-called 'field' watches – for use in the field – were, by definition, simple, affordable, tough, reliable and highly legible. Hamilton's A-11 is arguably the definition of the form.

The highly practical, user-friendly nature of the field watch made it a template for many 'outdoorsy' and sports watches to follow, from the Timex MK1 to the Rolex Explorer.

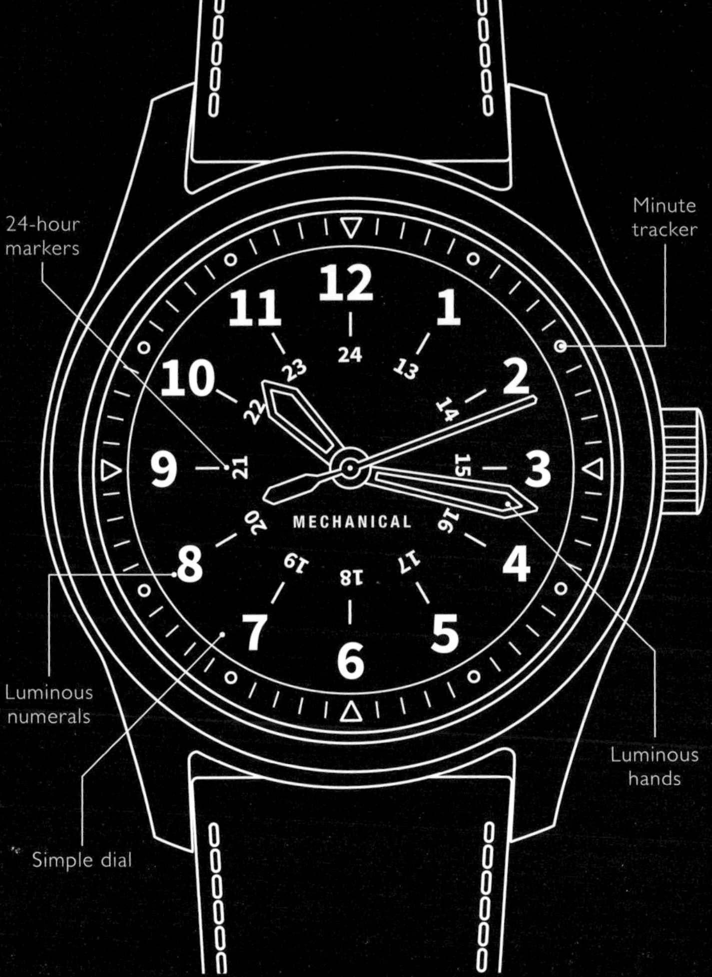
24-hour markers
Minute tracker
MECHANICAL
Luminous numerals
Luminous hands
Simple dial

A POSTWAR BOOM

With today's watch market dominated by a handful of names, it can be hard to imagine that, up until the 1970s, there were very many more brands. Originality in design is always a primary driver for gaining recognition and the two or so decades that followed World War II (1939–45) are cited as the golden age of watch design, with the introduction of a bold use of colour, graphics, materials and case shape.

International product design was enjoying a postwar consumer boom. Rising disposable incomes made the wearing of a watch normal for most men, if not yet most women, with many keen to buy a watch primarily for the way it looked. The Swiss watch industry, in particular, enjoyed advances in manufacturing capability and expanding markets at a time before the demands of mass-marketing edged out all but the most upscale of brands. And, crucially, before the Japanese commercialization of quartz technology wiped out all but the most prescient or hardy of mechanical watchmakers.

Watch designs of the period, among them groundbreaking creations from visionary product designers such as Roger Tallon, François de Baschmakoff or Richard Arbib were expressive and progressive. For example, Hamilton's Elvis Presley–

AMIDA
DIGITAL
AMIDA
DIGITAL
SWISS
AMIDA

approved Ventura (1957) had a triangular face; the 1970s Itraco Directime had a futuristic case with integrated bracelet and a mechanical jump- hour digital display; the Desotos Cuffbuster chronograph of 1972 had a case that sat almost entirely to the right side of its strap, allowing the display to poke out visibly beyond a shirt cuff; and the Amida Digitrend (1976), a new generation driver's watch, had the display angled so that it was visible when holding on to a steering wheel. It looks simple, but the numerals had to be printed backwards on to a rotating disc, then reflected through a clear plastic prism to be seen the right way round.

Many such watches are now collector's pieces from long-since defunct makers, though it's telling that many of the watches considered to be the most iconic today came out of this optimistic and imaginative period in watch design.

PAGE 26: French industrial designer Roger Tallon.
OPPOSITE: Amida wristwatches, 1971.

THE QUARTZ CRISIS

But then came what those in the watch industry refer to as the 'quartz crisis': the advent of battery-powered, quartz technology, first explored in Switzerland at the end of the 1960s and later popularized by Japanese watch companies such as Seiko.

Quartz movements were more reliable than mechanical ones, considerably more precise, more robust and – in the long term, thanks to innovative Japanese brands Citizen and Casio, mass-production methods and the leveraging of the Japanese electronics industry – much cheaper. Inevitably, small watch manufacturers were unable to compete and the market for mechanical watches was decimated. Around two-thirds of employees in the Swiss industry eventually lost their jobs.

A number of the bigger, mostly Swiss, watch manufacturers embraced quartz, but a battery-powered movement sat uneasily in a prestige case. It was only by competing with the Japanese at their own game, through the groundbreaking creation of Swatch, that the Swiss watch industry was able slowly to bounce back, albeit with greater conservatism in design and with marketing to the fore.

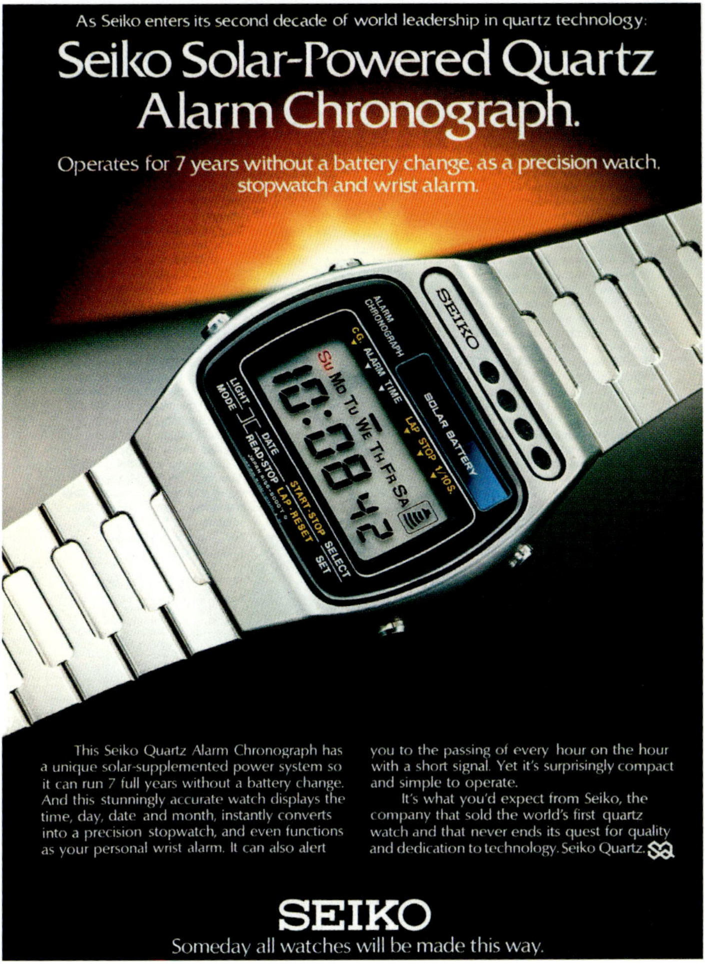

ABOVE: Seiko's 1979 solar-powered quartz alarm chronograph. By the time of its issue, Seiko was the world's largest watch company.

THE RISE OF THE GROUPS

The Swiss mechanical watch industry survived the onslaught of quartz largely through the efforts of two men. In the late 1970s, watchmaker Ernst Thomke drove consolidation: SSIH, owner of Omega, and ASUAG, owner of Longines, joined forces; ASUAG underwent a radical restructuring that saw its movement-manufacturing division reborn as ETA (now manufacturing analogue quartz movements, too).

Then, in the early 1980s, management consultant Nicolas Hayek combined ASUAG and SSIH under one new umbrella company, SMH, with all movement manufacturing for any brand in its portfolio given to ETA. Hayek took a further, radical and visionary step, competing directly with quartz watch manufacturers through the creation of Swatch. It is no exaggeration to say that this move rescued the industry. In 1998, Hayek renamed SMH the Swatch Group, now home to a diverse portfolio of watch brands, from the historically important Breguet, Blancpain and Glashütte to the mass-market Certina, Hamilton and Swatch. Further consolidation followed, with five companies now accounting for over three-quarters of all Swiss watch sales, including Richemont and LVMH.

ABOVE: Breitling Navitimer, 1993. Brands acquired by Breitling include Universal Genève (2023) and Gallet (2025).

TOP: HYT has developed a system that uses coloured liquids to indicate the time.
BOTTOM: Urwerk has a distinctive 'satellite' time display system.

INDEPENDENT MAKERS

While the brand giants of the watch industry command much of the limelight, many of the most respected makers remain small, independent operations known only to connoisseurs. The 'handmade' nature of their timepieces is sufficient to draw high-rolling customers, often surpassing the quality of better-known brands. And lower operational costs – coupled with the ability to turn a profit making relatively very few pieces – plus a long waiting list of eager clients, means they are freer to push design innovation, movement creation, watchmaking craft and use of materials to the limit.

Companies such as HYT, Urwerk and Ressence, for example, have developed innovative systems unique to their brands. Other watchmakers – Fiona Kruger, MB&F, Vianney Halter, François Junod and Stepan Sarpaneva, among them – have won plaudits for distinctive aesthetics, from skull-shaped watches, to the creative use of Super-LumiNova, among other progressive ideas. Others still, such as Roger Smith, Kari Voutilainen, Peter Speake-Marin, Bart and Tom Grönefeld and F.P. Journe, are admired simply for the excellence of their watchmaking.

THE WATCH IN POPULAR CULTURE

Entire brands have, at times, found a place in popular culture, often the result of behind-the-scenes marketing deals. Perhaps the most important pop-cultural association in history is that of the James Bond cinematic franchise and Omega since 1995, even if the character in Ian Fleming's novels (and some of the earlier films) wore a Rolex.

It helps that the watch, as a prop, proves to be an important plot device thanks to the spy gadgetry secreted within it. But the idea that having a presence in the movies pays well in terms of raised public profile is not lost on many watchmakers. Arnold Schwarzenegger wore a Seiko H558-5000 in *Commando* (1985) and *Predator* (1987); and the watch was subsequently nicknamed the 'Arnie' by fans. Rolex often sponsors the Oscars, and Audemars Piguet sponsors golf tournaments.

The brand power of many watchmakers as globally recognized status symbols also sees a long history of them being referenced in hip-hop and rap lyrics. Rolex is likely the most quoted watch brand in rap lyrics, with Patek Philippe also particularly prominent in the 2010s and beyond.

TOP: James Bond has worn an Omega since 1995.
BOTTOM: (Left) Steve McQueen wore a TAG Heuer Monaco in *Le Mans* (1971); (right) Schwarzenegger on the set of *Commando*.

THE VINTAGE MARKET

The vintage watch world has boomed since the turn of the century. Vintage watches sell because they are rare, unusual and aesthetically interesting. But they also embody a romance or nostalgia of the kind that watch brands themselves have explored by reissuing designs from their archives. If contemporary watches offer the talking points of movement, construction, function and design, vintage watches offer all that, plus the wonders of very small differences. One vintage Rolex, for example, might be valued much more highly than an otherwise identical piece, simply because two lines of type on its dial are in red. That's a 'double red' to those in the know. Others talk of 'ghost bezels', 'tropical dials' and 'pumpkin lumes', all desirable indicators of aging in a vintage watch.

The appreciation of vintage watches mirrors that of other collectibles, where being unrefurbished is important and provenance is key. In 2017, a 'Paul Newman' Daytona (a Rolex named after the man most closely associated with it) sold for US$17.75m, making it the most expensive wristwatch ever sold at the time. But then this was the motherlode: Paul Newman had actually once owned the watch in question.

ABOVE: Paul Newman was awarded a 1993 Rolex Daytona in 1995 when he became the oldest person to win the 24 Hours of Daytona race.

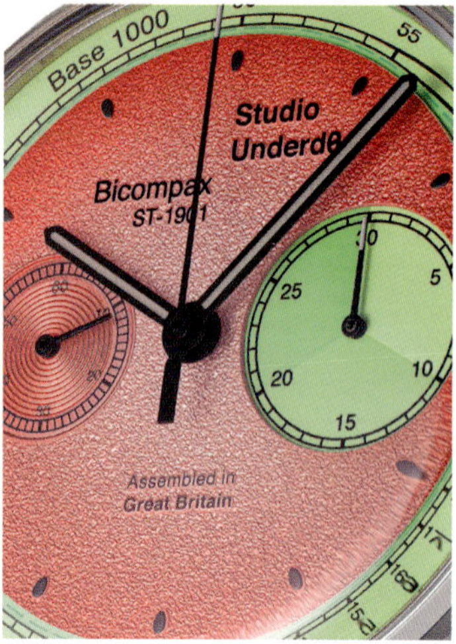

TOP: Prizewinning 37.09 Bluefin from Horologer MING.
BOTTOM: Watermelon and Boiled Egg from Studio Underd0g.

THE BIRTH OF THE MICROBRAND

There was a time when the Swatch Group's movement manufacturer ETA supplied its products to anyone: an ETA movement was the choice for many brands. But by the turn of the millennium the Swatch Group began to tighten controls over the watchmakers it supplied movements to. The move sparked a reaction, with several brands investing in their own 'in-house' movements, while other movement manufacturers, such as Sellita and Miyota pushed to fill the gap.

At the same time, the rise of online shopping reduced the need for bricks-and-mortar shops and social media lessened the need for huge advertising budgets. The impact on the watch industry was likely the most profound since the quartz crisis, giving rise to what some might term the watch 'microbrand'.

Consequently, the 21st century has seen a flourishing of adventurous, independent, mechanical watch companies able to find enough customers to be profitable. Often they are more adventurous than the brand giants. For example, British brand Studio Underdog employs a trend-setting use of colour, while Italy's Furlan Marri and Malaysia's Horologer MING have both won prestigious design prizes.

URWERK
sec
EMC

KEY CRAFTS AND TECHNOLOGIES

THE MECHANICAL MOVEMENT

The mechanism, known as the movement, that drives a watch today is a direct descendent of the very first horological mechanisms found in timepieces, and is little changed in essence. It uses a coiled, twisted metal spring – the mainspring – contained in a barrel and wound tight. Originally this was done through the turning of a key; later it was achieved via the crown, a wheel on the outside of the case that is attached to the movement via a stem.

This mainspring releases energy as it uncoils, which is transferred through a series of gears to the balance wheel, a weighted, oscillating wheel that, in turn, is linked to and regulated by a brake-like device called the escapement. The escapement periodically releases a gear train that advances the hands forward steadily and precisely to record the passing of hours, minutes and seconds.

The earliest watch movements were made of mostly circular parts mounted on a broadly circular brass main plate, with the movement of the hands around the dial also being circular. Hence, most watch cases have been round. Despite being fundamentally unchanging in their basics,

12
1
2
3
4
5
6
7
8
9
10
11

PAGE 42: Urwerk's EMC model.
PAGE 45: A disassembled watch.
ABOVE: The mechanical watch movement up close.

watch movements have made advances to improve their functionality or accuracy. As early as 1777, for example, Swiss watchmaker Abraham-Louis Perrelet devised the first 'automatic' movement, using a weighted rotor that moved freely according to the motion of the wearer's wrist, winding the mainspring as it did so. (The technology was not patented or produced commercially until 1923.) Similarly, the coaxial escapement, devised by English watchmaker George Daniels in the 1970s, and considered one of the greatest advances in watchmaking of recent times, significantly reduces friction, improving accuracy.

An automatic watch constantly replenishes its mainspring with energy. How long a nonautomatic or hand-wound watch will run for before it needs re-winding is known as the power reserve. For modern mechanical watches this is around 40 hours, though some watchmakers have made advances allowing for watches with power reserves of anywhere between a week and, as the name of Lange & Söhne's Lange 31 suggests, a full month.

Most watchmakers buy in their movements from specialist movement manufacturers, with ETA, Miyota, Sellita and Ronda among the largest. Still, many aspire to design and produce their own movements in-house, where they are known as 'manufacture movements'.

SKELETON

The concept of the skeletonized watch – of cutting away the dial to reveal the movement below – has roots in 18th century France. It was there, in the 1760s, that watchmaker Jean-Antoine Lépine reworked the plates and bridges of a movement to make his pocket watches considerably thinner than those of his competitors. Lépine's format also looked rather pretty, inspiring his father-in-law and former watchmaking teacher André-Charles Caron to open up the case. In doing so, owners could see – and show others – just what a miniature marvel the movement was.

The fad didn't last and the idea was all but forgotten until the 1970s, when the advent of quartz threatened the survival of the mechanical watch industry. What better way to counter the march of technology than by highlighting the craft intrinsic to a mechanical movement, in a sense making its anachronism central to its appeal?

Getting this right was no mean feat. The function of a movement depends on a careful distribution of mass and removing material, even by fractions of a millimetre, putting this in potential jeopardy. It became a new benchmark of the watchmaker's art. Watchmakers Armin Strom and Jochen Benzinger soon built reputations in the field, and big brands followed.

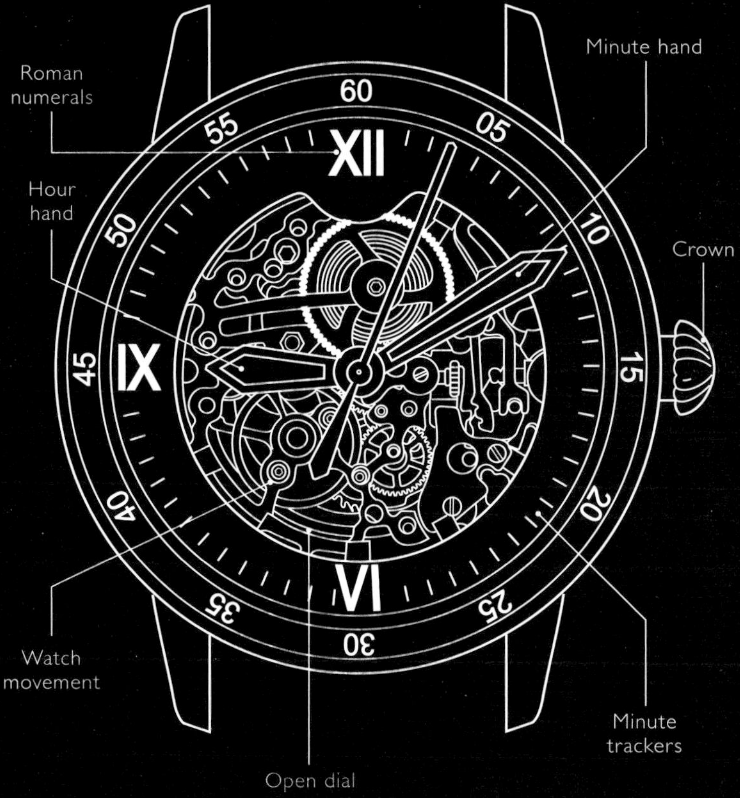
Roman numerals
Hour hand
Watch movement
Open dial
Minute hand
Crown
Minute trackers
60
05
10
15
20
25
30
35
40
45
50
55
XII
IX
VI

BENCHMARKS OF COMPLEXITY

The basic mechanical watch movement is a simple one, giving hour, minute and, sometimes, seconds, but watchmakers have long built in additional functionalities, known in the industry as 'complications'. A date display is a commonplace complication, but often as a testament to their watchmaking skills, elite watchmakers seek to build far more sophisticated complications into their designs, frequently including several in a single watch. The true utility of these may be open to debate – this is typically more about testing the boundaries of what is possible both without electronics and in such a confined space – but complications exponentially increase the prestige of a watch.

Advanced complications might include an annual calendar, first developed by Patek Philippe in 1996, and the minute repeater, which allows a watch to chime the time on demand using different tones for hours, quarter hours and minutes. Scaling this complication down to work at wristwatch size, to produce a pleasing sound that's also clearly audible at a distance, has proven one of the most intractable challenges in watchmaking.

ABOVE: Patek Philippe's Grandmaster Chime (2016) had 20 complications, requiring over 1,500 components. They included a leap-year cycle, a moon phase and a four-digit year display.

ABOVE: A 1929 advert for Rolex's Oyster. In 1910, the model received the first official chronometer certification for a wristwatch.

THE RACE FOR PRECISION

In 1735, British watchmaker John Harrison developed a 'marine chronometer'. It gave ships an accurate onboard clock, allowing navigators to determine longitude and so work out their position at sea. This made global exploration and trade possible.

In the late 19th and early 20th centuries, the use of the word 'chronometer' on the dial of a timepiece meant submitting the movement to a testing facility such as the UK's Kew Observatory or Switzerland's Neuchatel Observatory. Today, most Swiss chronometers are certified by the COSC (*Contrôle Officiel Suisse des Chronomètres*), which puts applicant movements through 15 days of tests. Yet some watchmakers claim their technological advances mean their timekeeping standards surpass those set by COSC, and they want this acknowledged. Consequently, some brands have established their own in-house certification programmes in addition to those provided by COSC: Patek Philippe applies its own Patek Philippe Seal, Rolex its Superlative Chronometer rating, Omega its Master Chronometer rating, Grand Seiko its Special Standard . . . and so the race for ever-greater precision goes on.

ADVENTURES IN CIRCUITRY

A quartz movement uses a battery to produce a current in a circuit, which causes a piece of quartz to vibrate at precisely 32,768 times a second and to convert the vibrations into a one-second electric pulse. At its very best, a mechanical watch might beat at 108,000 vibrations *per hour*. As such, a quartz movement operates to within an accuracy of +/–5 seconds a month, whereas a mechanical watch might achieve +/–5 seconds per day. Such a high-tech system deserved a high-tech style: quartz went hand in hand with the development of LED (later LCD) digital displays.

The compactness of quartz also led to some world-beating creations: at just 1.98 mm thick, the Concord Delirium (1979) was, thanks to a specially developed quartz movement, the thinnest watch ever made; a decade later, Seiko introduced its 9A85, at 0.85 mm thick, still the world's thinnest. Further innovations include Bulova's Precision, which allowed for a sweeping seconds hand; Grand Seiko's 9F, where each crystal is individually grown to match the integrated circuit with which it will work; and Seiko's Spring Drive, which uses a quartz crystal–based control mechanism to regulate the way the spring unwinds.

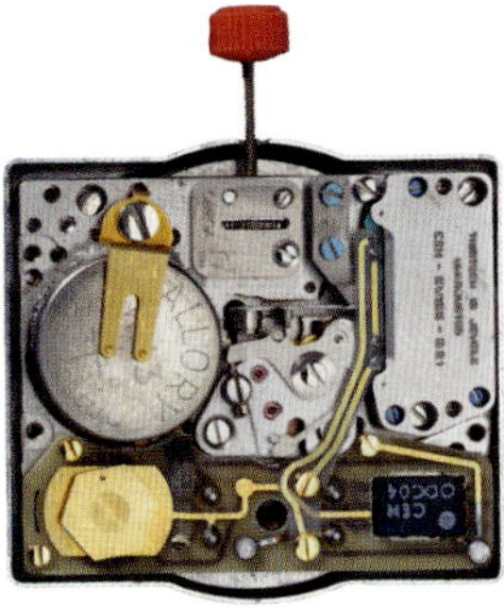

ABOVE: (Top left) A quartz watch movement; (top right) the Seiko Astron; (bottom) comparing a mechanical movement (left) with a quartz movement (right).

DUAL TIME

The 19th century boom in global trade led to the International Meridian Conference of 1884. It established Greenwich Mean Time (GMT), the division of the globe into 24 longitudinal time zones.

In time, this lead to the demand for a practical device that could be set to display the time in whatever zone you happened to be, as well as that of your 'home' zone. Watchmaker Louis Cottier is credited with the creation of the first, highly complex, 'universal time' movement, in 1931. It featured a rotating bezel depicting international cities to represent the time zones. But it was Swiss watchmaker Glycine that, in 1953, launched the first commercial watch able to track two 24-hour time zones: the Airman, which used a moveable bezel allowing the calibration of a second 24-hour time display. The watch was named deliberately to appeal to pilots of the new international jet-setting era. Indeed, the Airman was first issued to pilots of the Pan Am airline.

In 1954, Rolex launched its own variant, the GMT-Master, with a second hour hand indicating the time against a 24-hour bezel with two colours to indicate AM and PM. Though subtle, this difference became the industry standard, as epitomized by Seiko's 1968 Navigator Timer.

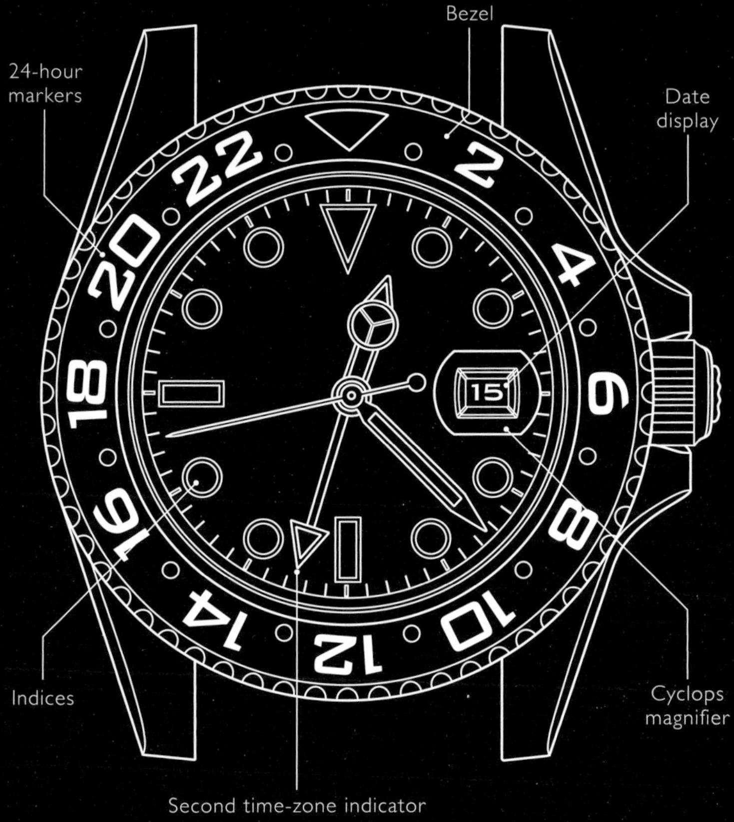
Bezel
24-hour markers
Date display
Indices
Cyclops magnifier
Second time-zone indicator

ABOVE: (Top) A luminescent dial; (bottom) luminescent numbers.

LUMINESCENCE

That a watch should be visible at night is an obvious benefit, but not one easily achieved without battery power and bulb. In the case of mechanical watches, the earliest attempts, soon after World War I, deployed radium-based paints, despite their radioactivity.

Radium's use was widely banned in 1968, largely replaced by tritium. But with a half-life of 12 years, tritium's glow was not permanent. Replacing it led to the invention of Super-LumiNova by Japanese chemist Kenzo Nemoto in 1993. Subsequently licensed and developed by Swiss family company RC Tritec, it now dominates the watch industry. Super-LumiNova has to be exposed to a light source to charge up its ability to emit light. Its maker is constantly juggling chemical parameters to alter its decay characteristics: you can have a high brightness initially with lower performance over time, or vice versa, but not both. Grade by grade, however, this luminous material has improved such that its latest incarnations are magnitudes brighter than previous ones.

Tritium is being explored again, this time contained in tiny glass tubes, as used by Ball Watch and Luminox. It's a hundred times brighter than Super-LumiNova and does not require pre-charging by exposure to a light source.

WATERPROOFING

Early on, the idea of a wristwatch as opposed to a pocket watch met with scepticism, because it was exposed to conditions that could seriously hamper its functionality, not least the ingress of water. Making a watch water-resistant consequently became an objective for many manufacturers.

Early developments began in the 1920s, when Swiss maker Francis Baumgartner developed the screw-down caseback, effectively enclosing the movement in a watertight compartment. In 1925, two Swiss watchmakers, Perregaux and Peret, devised a screw stem system that allowed the crown, the other critical point of entry for water, to form a watertight seal. It was this technology that, a year later, saw Rolex launch the Oyster, claiming the model to be the first dust- and water-resistant watch.

By the early 1930s, when Omega launched its first diving watch, the Marine, the idea of a water-resistant wristwatch had finally taken hold. But it would take the advent of the professional diving watch to take waterproofing to new extremes, encouraging, as it did, the development of synthetic seals and, on deeper water models at least, a helium escape valve to let out compressed gases and prevent the watch from literally exploding after a rapid ascent.

ABOVE: A 1994 advert for the Citizen Promaster professional sports watch.

DIVING WATCH

he safe diving limit for amateurs is 40 m (130 ft) below he surface, but the development of the Aqua-Lung by egendary diver Jacques Cousteau and engineer Emile Gagnan, in 1942, led to the birth of scuba diving for eisure, in turn setting watchmakers the challenge of creating the ultimate form of macho tool: the diving watch. Its creation took decades of development, starting with the demands of the military – for example, Panerai created an outsized diving watch for talian commandos during World War II.

In 1953, one of the earliest deep-sea tests saw bathyscaphe descend to 3,150 m (10,335 ft) with a pecially constructed watch strapped to it. That same year, after extensive trials with professional divers, Rolex launched its Submariner. Capable of reaching depths up to 100 m (330 ft), it was the first model with the watch type's signature detail: a rotating bezel.

Today's diving watches are small marvels of engineering. With pressures at sea level of one atmosphere (1 atm – the equivalent of 1 kg per cm^2/ 5 lb per in^2), a diving watch is subjected to an additional 1 atm every 10 m (33 ft) down. The pressures uickly become huge and temperatures plummet

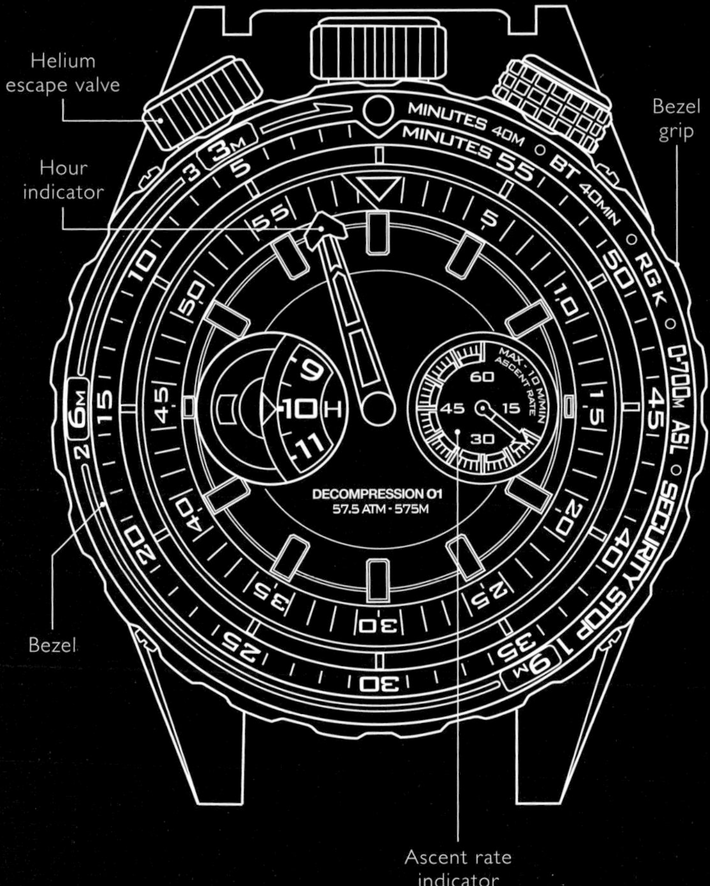
Helium escape valve
Hour indicator
Bezel
Bezel grip
Ascent rate indicator
MINUTES
MINUTES 40M
MINUTES 55
BT 40MIN
RGK
0-700M ASL
SECURITY STOP 1
DECOMPRESSION 01
57.5 ATM - 575M
MAX - 10 M/MIN ASCENT RATE

THE DECORATIVE ARTS

The earliest watches were not merely tools for telling the time. They were often highly decorative, as much pieces of jewellery as wonders of micromechanics. They featured highly skilled handcrafts, many of which – rare as they are – remain championed today by artisanal brands such as Cartier and Hermès.

The Swiss refer to these painstaking crafts as the *metiers d'art* and they include lacquering, gold cloisonné, marquetry, guilloche, filigree and enamelling. Long-forgotten forms of decoration, perhaps only seen in museum pieces, are occasionally investigated and revived. Cartier, for example, brought back granulation, an art form that peaked with the Etruscans, involving fusing gold granules onto a gold plate to create a relief.

New *metiers d'art* emerge, too. For example, Cartier also devised a form of floral marquetry dial decoration that sees preserved petals set into slivers of wood, which are then hand-carved to create elaborate designs. The first model used rose petals to mimic parrot feathers on a special version of its Ballon Bleu de Cartier watch. Hermès used straw marquetry on a special edition of its 1978 Arceau model.

ABOVE: In a series of watches paying homage to the great civilizations of antiquity, Vacheron Constantin reproduce iconic works from the Louvre Museum as miniature appliqué elements.

ADVANCED MATERIALS

A watch's prestige was once, in part, underscored by the precious metal from which its case was made: gold and platinum spoke of quality, tradition and heritage. But the 21st century has seen a radical shift towards making the wristwatch feel modern again through the use of advanced materials.

If movement components made of silicon are increasingly deployed to enhance precision, case design now deploys titanium, carbon fibre, forged carbon, ceramics, sapphire crystal, carbon glass and bulk metallic glass, but also proprietary hybrid materials such as Audemars Piguet's Chroma Forged Composite, Ulysse Nardin's Carbonium®, IWC's Ceratanium and Tag Heuer's TH-Polylight.

Such materials, as well as production methods borrowed from the aviation and automotive industries, in particular, have been used to make cases of exceptional lightness, durability and scratch resistance; even to give them hypoallergenic properties. These new materials also offer new aesthetics in the way they feel in the hand, in how they catch the light, or allow for distinctive effects (forged carbon's marbling, for example).

ABOVE: Ulysse Nardin's Freak X Gumball 3000 – Edition 2
with Carbonium® hour-disc.

10
ROLEX
ROLEX
OYSTER PERPETUAL DATE
OFFICIALLY CERTIFIED
40

THE BRANDS TO KNOW

VACHERON CONSTANTIN

With much time comes much expertise. Founded by Jean-Marc Vacheron in Geneva in 1755, Vacheron Constantin is the world's oldest continuously operational watchmaker. Alongside Patek Philippe and Audemars Piguet, it is considered to be one of the so-called 'Holy Trinity' of elite makers.

After taking over in 1785, Jean-Marc's son Abraham built the company's reputation as a maker of some of the first pocket watches with complications. Francois Constantin joined the business in the early 1800s. Technical director Georges-Auguste Leschot joined in 1839 and invented the pantograph. The first means of making movement components with reliably identical dimensions, it was once credited as being the single most important breakthrough in the development of Swiss watchmaking. So began a long history of making elegantly classical watches, such as Vacheron Constantin's Jorg Hysek–designed 222 (1977) sports model, but also some of the most technically accomplished, too. In 2025, Vacheron Constantin made the Solaria Ultra Grande Complication (2025), with 1,521 components, the most complicated wristwatch made to date.

ABOVE: The Traditionnelle exemplifies the brand's tradition of making elegant wristwatches of the highest technical specification.
PAGE 68: Rolex Submariner.

BREGUET

Legendary Swiss clock and watchmaker Abraham-Louis Breguet is credited with many inventions. He established his business in Paris, in 1775, after apprenticing with the pioneering Jean-Antoine Lépine. Supplier to the French Navy, Breguet also developed the self-winding '*perpetual*' watch, the first 'elastic suspension', shock-resistant timepiece (1790), the tourbillon mechanism (French for 'whirlwind'; 1795), the detached constant force escapement (1798) and the double-barrel marine chronometer (1798). He also devised a curious mechanism, dubbed the tactful watch, that allowed the user to check the approximate time on their pocket watch by touch alone. A Breguet creation from 1810–1812 – widely considered to be the first watch ever designed to be worn on a wrist – inspired the brand's Reine de Naples collection.

Over the centuries, various royal figures, heads of state, captains of industry and luminaries, among them Marie Antoinette, Louis XVIII, Napoleon I, Alexander Dumas, Queen Victoria and, later, Rossini, Rothschild, Bugatti and Churchill were all Breguet customers. Then as now, such clients were drawn not just to the complexity of these timepieces, but to their timeless style.

ABOVE: Breguet 5157, the blue steel hands are a signature design element, created by Abraham-Louis Breguet around 1783.

ABOVE: Designed by engineer René-Alfred Chauvot, the Reverso was created in response to a challenge from British polo players.

JAEGER-LECOULTRE

Jaeger-LeCoultre was founded in 1833, when Antoine LeCoultre set up his workshop in Le Sentier, in the Swiss Vallée de Joux – renowned today for the number of high-end watchmakers located there. The company can now claim over 350 patents and 500 complicated calibres. Among its technical triumphs are the Calibre 101, the world's smallest mechanical movement (a record held since 1929) and the Master Compressor Extreme LAB (2007), a movement designed to operate entirely without lubricant yet without deterioration to parts and performance.

There have been many memorable timepieces, from the Atmos mantle clock (1928) – still an official gift of the Swiss government to foreign state guests – to the Memovox (1950), the first watch to offer a reliable mechanical alarm, and the Futurematic (1951), the first watch without a visible crown. Yet the Jaeger-LeCoultre brand itself has almost been superseded by one particular model: the Art Deco-style, 'two-faced' Reverso (1931), which was designed with a mechanism that allows the case to be slid across and flipped over, protecting the watch's dial during strenuous activity.

PATEK PHILIPPE

One of the last remaining, independent, family-owned watchmakers, Patek Philippe represents the pinnacle of series production watchmaking. It was founded in 1839 by two Polish immigrants, salesman Antoine Norbert de Patek and watchmaker Franciszek Czapek, becoming Patek Philippe in 1851 when Czapek left and French watchmaker Jean Adrien Philippe joined.

One of the few companies to design and make its watches entirely in-house, the legendary brand has a number of firsts to its name, not least, in 1868, the creation of the first Swiss wristwatch. The 1880s saw patents for a precision regulator and a perpetual calendar; 1922, the first split-seconds chronograph; 1925, the first wristwatch with a perpetual calendar; 1956, the first all-electronic clock, and so it goes on.

Many models are considered to be classics. The oval Golden Ellipse (1968) challenged conventions of form, while the Nautilus (1976) and the Aquanaut (1997) both rewrote ideas of what a luxury sports watch could be. Among its much admired complication watches are the Sky Moon Tourbillon (2001) and the 20-complication Grandmaster Chime (2016). So esteemed are its watches that its legendary slogan, 'You never really own a Patek Philippe. You merely look after it for the next generation,' rings true.

ABOVE: Inspired by the portholes of transatlantic ships, the Nautilus was created by esteemed watch designer Gérald Genta.

DRESS WATCH

Until the 1920s and 30s, most watches were elaborate in style, an outward expression of the maker's prestige. What might be considered the archetypal watch today – medium-sized, relatively plain, slim enough to slide under a shirt cuff, with a two-hand hour-and-minute display – had yet to be invented.

In 1932, watchmaker Patek Philippe launched such a watch, later naming it the Calatrava. Designed by horologist David Penney, it was stylistically matter of fact, using baton markers rather than Arabic numerals, and a central seconds display.

At the time of its launch, the Calatrava marked a distinct break from the ornate watch aesthetics that had come before it, and this made it pioneering. It drove the idea of the wristwatch as an eminently wearable accessory for the middle-class professional. There was still a focus on craft – the markings of the seconds subdial, for example, were engraved onto the plate, laboriously painted in black enamel and fired – but it was also one of the company's most affordable, and so accessible, wristwatches to date. Inevitably, this less-is-more approach would find many imitators, from the Rolex Cellini to Omega's De Ville. The label 'dress watch' might suggest 'dressing up', but really it implies a more everyday, all-occasions model

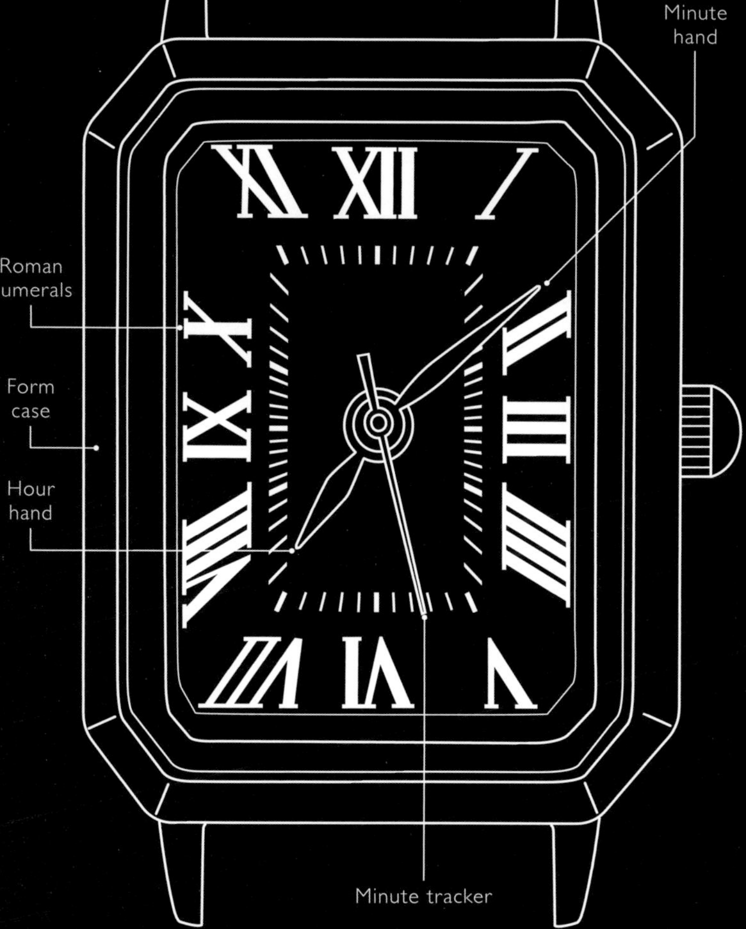
Minute hand
Roman umerals
Form case
Hour hand
Minute tracker

© Lange Uhren GmbH

© Lange Uhren GmbH

© Lange Uhren GmbH

A. LANGE & SÖHNE

A. Lange & Söhne's is a story interrupted. The prestigious German company, established in 1845 and a pioneer of the three-quarter plate and a proprietary lever escapement, among other movement advances, was relaunched in 1990 after a 45-year interlude, during which time the company was expropriated by the communist authorities of former East Germany. After German reunification, Walter Lange – great-grandson of founder Ferdinand Adolph Lange – was able to take ownership once more.

The company has created several watchmaking innovations, including a now signature, outsized date display and an off-centre time read-out. Four models launched in 1994 included the asymmetric Lange 1, to immediate critical and commercial success. Since that time, the brand – based in Glashütte, Saxony – has created a series of refined watchmaking classics, notably the Datograph flyback chronograph (1999) and the Zeitwerk (2009), with a mechanical digital display. It has also achieved the status of elite watchmaker, able to make only a few thousand pieces to its high standard each year.

FROM LEFT TO RIGHT: A. Lange & Söhne's Zeitwerk Date, the asymmetric Lange 1 Daymatic Honeygold and the Datograph Up/Down "Hampton Court Edition".

ULYSSE NARDIN

Though founded in 1846, and primarily a maker of world-class marine chronometers, Ulysse Nardin is notable for its most recent history.

When, in 2023, the Grand Prix d'Horlogerie de Genève, the Oscars of Swiss watchmaking, named Ulysse Nardin's Freak One the winner of its 'iconic' category, it was in recognition of the latest iteration of a model that, since its launch in 2001, had shifted the way watches were both conceived and, in turn, perceived. Here was a watch with no crown – the display is adjusted using the bezel, the watch wound using the casebook. Further, here was a watch with no dial or hands, utilizing the movement itself to display the time, almost as a kind of kinetic art. It was also the first watch with a silicium escapement.

This Freak represented a shift away from a classical approach to watchmaking to one that prioritized innovation – a shift driven by Swiss businessman Rolf Schnyder, who acquired the company in 1983. A Ludwig Oechslin-devised Trilogy of Time watches – launched in 1985 with the Astrolabium, the first astronomical wristwatch, followed by the Planetarium and Tellurium – set the industry pace for bold complications that Ulysse Nardin would follow with an equally bold approach to materials and design.

ABOVE: The iconic Freak ONE OPS has accumulated 35 patents since its launch in 2001.

CARTIER

'I wear a Tank because it's the watch to wear,' intoned Andy Warhol in the 1960s, some 40 years after the launch of the brand's most famous model, in 1919.

Founded in 1847, Cartier was best known for making jewellery, a tradition that continues to this day. When Alfred Cartier took over the business from his father Louis-François in 1874, timepieces were in his plans for expansion. Alfred's son Louis entered the firm in 1899 with even greater enthusiasm and determined that Cartier should make its own pocket watch; by 1904, the first wrist-worn watch, the Santos, was in production. Signing a deal with Jaeger-LeCoultre and, later, other manufacturers for the supply of movements, Cartier went on to produce a long roster of cultish classics.

The Tank was one of six pieces in a radical new style, designed to capture the look of the newfangled war machines of World War I, and of the Renault FT-17 tank in particular. Many models feature Cartier's signature blue sapphire cabochon crown – not just the Tank, but the Crash (1967), the elliptical Baignoire or 'bathtub' (1973), the Pasha (1985) and the voluminous Ballon Bleu (2007). The 21st century saw Cartier pioneer a high-tech concept watch, the ID One (2009), conceived as a single piece of carbon crystal.

TOP: Jewel-encrusted Ballon Bleu. BOTTOM (left): Advert for the Tank, 1990s; (right) the Baignoire, with its signature oval silhouette.

ABOVE: A 1967 Crash. Produced in various iterations, and very low numbers, the Crash is highly sought-after.

CARTIER CRASH

Maker: Cartier | *Watch*: Crash | *Launched*: 1967

HISTORY

Said to be inspired by a Cartier Maxi Oval watch after it had melted in a car accident, the Crash was in fact the brainchild of Jean-Jacques Cartier and Rupert Emmerson, perhaps inspired by Salvador Dalí's Surrealist painting, *The Persistence of Memory*.

FUNCTIONALITY

The dial involved positioning the numbers on an irregular shape, yet with the hands still telling the time. It proved as much of a challenge as the case-making and had to be redesigned several times. It met the objective of being different, however; actor Stewart Granger returned his for being too different!

IMPACT

A bold departure from watchmaking's attachment to symmetry, and chiming with the counterculture of the 1960s, the Crash revealed a new paradigm in watch design and would become a blue-chip investment piece.

TAG HEUER

Edouard Heuer founded his small Swiss watchmaking business in 1860, slowly building a reputation as a maker of reliable stopwatches. His became the first company to patent a chronograph, in 1882, going on to win the first international prize for a chronograph at the 1889 Paris Exposition. By 1920 Heuer was the official supplier of chronographs to the Olympic Games and over the subsequent decades, would invent ever more precise and specialist pieces.

Among Heuer's chronograph models were several of avant-garde design, notably the Autavia (1961), its name a portmanteau of 'automobile' and 'aviation'; the Carrera (1963), a stripped-back, elegant model aimed at racing-car drivers; and the Monaco (1969). Heuer also became the brand of motorsports, providing chronographs to Ferrari's Formula 1 team from 1971. In 1985, private holding company Techniques d'Avant Garde (TAG) acquired a majority shareholding, resulting in a new TAG Heuer brand. Within seven years, it was the official timekeeper for Formula 1 as a whole, and went on to create more groundbreaking concept watches, notably the Monaco V4 (2004), the first belt-driven watch and the Mikrotimer Flying 1000 Concept (2011), the first mechanical watch able to measure 1/1,000th of a second.

ABOVE: Tiger Woods advertising the Tag Heuer Link Antenna X Automatic Chronograph, 2006.

IWC

Established as International Watch Company in Schaffhausen, Switzerland, in 1868, IWC's founder was American watchmaker Florentine-Ariosto Jones. Within a decade, however, Jones was back in the US and the company was in Swiss hands.

It subsequently gained a reputation, through its Calibre 52 (1893), as a maker of fine watches; it was the watch of choice for Winston Churchill and Pope Pius IX. From the 1930s, IWC became a specialist in aviation watches, notably with its high-legibility Big Pilot (1940) and series of Mark pieces (1936 to present). In 1939, two Lisbon watch importers asked IWC to produce a model celebrating Portugal's seafaring heritage. The resulting Portugieser model was an oversized timepiece, with pocket-watch movements in the spirit of navigational instruments.

Postwar, IWC became known for its development of a luxury take on tool watches in high-tech materials – for example, the Ingenieur (1955), initially developed as an antimagnetic watch for engineers became a benchmark in sports watches following a redesign by Gerald Genta in 1976. The company also mastered advanced complications following an agreement in 1949 to develop watches with Porsche, creating the titanium Ocean 2000 (1982).

TOP: The Ingenieur, following Genta's redesign.
BOTTOM: The Portugieser was a radical departure for watch design of the time.

TOP: Star Wheel, the first wristwatch with a wandering hours display.
BOTTOM: Code 11.59, with multi-layered case designs, double-curved crystals, and a distinctive optical effect.

AUDEMARS PIGUET

Jules Louis Audemars and friend Edward Auguste Piguet (AP) founded their watchmaking company in Le Brassus, Switzerland, in 1875. A decade later they had designed their first 'grande complication' pocket watch, introducing complex pieces to the market. At the 1889 Paris Exposition, they presented what was widely considered a masterpiece: a pocket watch with a split-second chronograph, perpetual calendar and minute repeater. AP was on its way to being considered one of the so-called 'Holy Trinity' of elite watchmakers (Patek Philippe and Vacheron Constantin being the others).

It even dabbled in the idea of the wristwatch long before most of its competitors, showcasing the world's first with a minute repeater in 1891, and making others under licence for a number of jewellers, including Tiffany. This progressive approach is best captured in the creation of its most famous product, the Royal Oak (1972) sports watch, the company's most popular model to date. Even so, AP continued its work in creating grand complications, including the first self-winding tourbillon, as well as important models Dual Time (1981), the 1990s Offshore line, the Star Wheel (1991), and its unconventional line Code 11.59 (from 2019).

ABOVE: The Royal Oak takes its name from a series of eight British Royal Navy ships named HMS *Royal Oak*.

AUDEMARS PIGUET ROYAL OAK

Maker: Audemars Piguet | *Watch*: Royal Oak | *Launched*: 1972

HISTORY

Designed overnight by Gérald Genta, designer of the Patek Philippe Nautilus, Pasha de Cartier and Omega Constellation, among others, the Royal Oak was the sports watch that first allowed stainless steel to be regarded as a high-end material at a time when the watch industry coveted gold and platinum.

FUNCTIONALITY

The Royal Oaks expresses its water-resistance both through its name and its looks. The integrated bracelet, octagonal, porthole-style bezel and surrounding outsized screws are said to have been inspired by those on an old-fashioned diving helmet.

IMPACT

When the Royal Oak was designed, Audemars Piguet boss Jacques-Louis Piguet thought it might sell 1,000 pieces. It became the company's all-time best-seller, kick-starting a trend for outsized watches and defining a new, luxury sports watch category.

BREITLING

Breitling's advertising phrase 'instruments for professionals' certainly makes sense if you are a pilot. The company's story goes back to 1884, when it was founded in St. Imier, Switzerland, by Leon Breitling.

In 1915, Leon's son conceived of the first chronograph. Having a particular association with aviation watches from the 1930s, Breitling has designed a number of pioneering pieces in this field. The first Chronomat watch (1942), proposed by Gaston's son, Willy, was the first chronograph to be fitted with a circular slide rule, and was one of the designs to win the company a long-standing sales relationship with the US armed forces. Other key pieces include the Navitimer (1952), dubbed a 'navigation computer', with a bezel arrangement that allowed a pilot to make all necessary calculations for a flight plan. NASA pioneer Scott Carpenter wore a Navitimer in space in 1962. Breitling's watches have always been driven by function over style: its Emergency (1995) model, for example, was the first wristwatch with an integrated emergency distress beacon. One was used to rescue two British pilots in 2003, after their helicopter crashed in Antarctica.

OPPOSITE: The Breitling Navitimer.

BREITLING
MPH
BASE
KM
1000 M
NAUT.
STAT.
SWISS
MADE

CHRONOGRAPH

In 1923, Gaston Breitling introduced the first wristwatch chronograph with a stop/start pusher. With its information-packed dial and playful buttons, it became a specialist tool for pilots, and was popular more widely for timing everything from artillery bombardments to motor races. Subsequent developments have seen the creation of incredibly precise mechanical chronographs. TAG Heuer's Mikrogirder, for example, is a concept piece capable of timing events to 1/2000th of a second.

What gave the chronograph appeal beyond professional application was the development of the first automatic version. Zenith had secretly been working on this idea since the early 1960s, and when its El Primero was finally launched, in 1969, it was groundbreaking. It allowed for the measurement of elapsed time to a then unheard of 1/10th of a second – literally the blink of an eye – with the central rotor, column wheel and other parts of the automatic movement having undergone remarkable miniaturization. The El Primero has remained in almost continuous production to this day and is still the most accurate chronograph in serial production, with more recent versions capable of clocking elapsed time to 1/100th of a second.

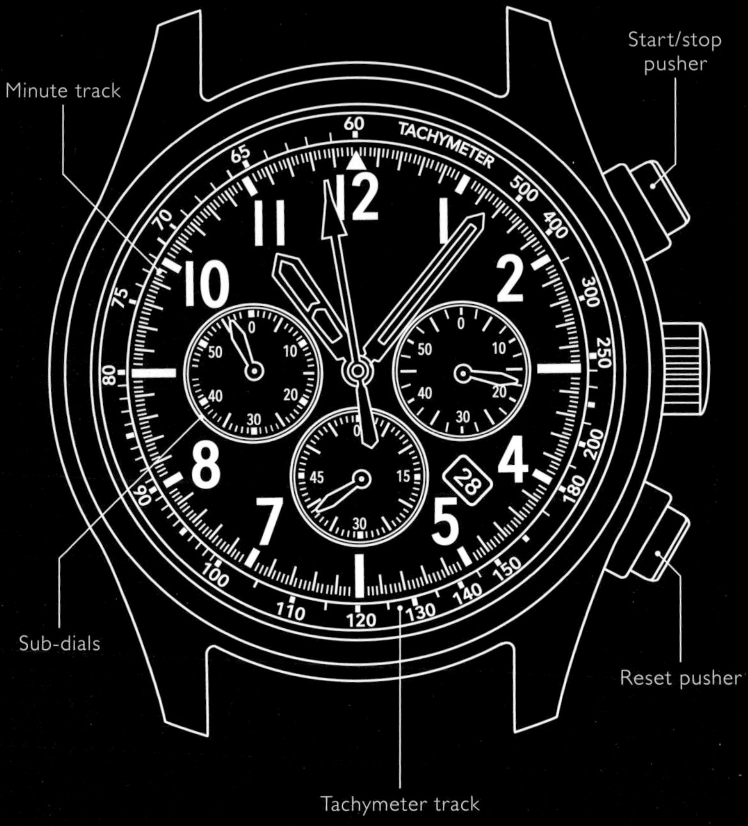
Minute track
Start/stop pusher
Sub-dials
Reset pusher
Tachymeter track

ABOVE: The Octo Finissimo series included history's thinnest tourbillon movement (1.95 mm) and thinnest self-winding watch (5.15 mm).

BULGARI

Like Cartier, Bulgari's heritage as a jeweller – established in Rome by the Greek silversmith Sotirios Voulgaris in 1884 – focused initially on heavily jewelled women's watches in the Art Deco style. By the 1940s, the company had begun to develop its own distinctive looks. A watch made as a special gift for its top clients in 1975, the Bulgari Roma gold digital watch, led to the launch of an analogue version for men two years later, the Bulgari Bulgari. The success of this watch encouraged Bulgari to establish a division in Switzerland in 1980, where it began acquiring watch companies with movement and dial-making capabilities, including Gérald Genta Haute Horlogerie.

It was quick to establish its own look, too: the Diagono (1988) brought a new boldness to how a watch might be branded, while the Aluminium (1998) was way ahead of the industry in its use of aluminium and rubber in a luxury product. Six years later, Bulgari unveiled its first grand complication, a tourbillon and, having been acquired itself by LVMH, the Octo (2012), a reworking of a Gérald Genta design.

Perhaps Bulgari's greatest contribution to high-end watchmaking, however, was its focus on super-thin watches, leading, from 2014, to a rapid series of seven world record–setting Octo Finissimo pieces.

SEIKO

In 1892, Kintaro Hattori and Tsuruhiko Yoshikawa launched a clock company called Seikosha, loosely meaning 'house of exquisite craftsmanship'. It created its first pocket watch in 1895, naming it Timekeeper to improve sales abroad. By 1913 it had launched the Laurel, its first wristwatch.

It was not until 1924 that the first watch carrying the Seiko name was launched. In 1956 the Seiko Marvel became the company's first watch with an in-house designed movement. In 1960 the company would launch another high-end line, the refined Grand Seiko. At the end of the decade, in 1969, Seiko's 5 Sports Speed Timer beat Swiss competitors to market with the first automatic chronograph.

That same year saw the first of a succession of seismic innovations that threatened to put an end to mechanical watches: the Astron, the world's first quartz wristwatch. More groundbreaking ideas would follow, among them the quartz movement of the AGS Kinetic (1988), which had an oscillating weight that converted motions of the wearer's wrist into the electricity needed to power it, and the Astron GPS Solar (2012), which adjusted itself to local time anywhere by taking signals from GPS satellites.

TOP: The high-tech Astron was initially pitched as a luxury model.
BOTTOM: The Grand Seiko exceeded standards set by the Swiss COCS.

GRADUE POUR 15 PULSATIONS
OMEGA
TACHYMETRE
OMEGA
PROFESSIONAL
OMEGA
AUTOMATIC CHRONOMETER
OMEGA
PROFESSIONAL
TACHYMÈTRE
OMEGA
PROFESSIONAL
TACHYMETRE

OMEGA

Omega holds the status of being one of the most outward-bound of Swiss watchmakers – rivalled only by Rolex. Omega watches having successfully faced the challenges of deep-sea diving, aviation, spaceflight, sport and – in fiction at least – espionage.

The boldness of its name no doubt helped; the company was established as Louis Brandt & Frere, pocket watch manufacturer, in 1894, but changed its name a few years later. In 1917 Omega, still a family firm under the charge of a quartet of Brandts, chose to invest in aviation, a decision that would pay handsomely when one of its chronographs, the Speedmaster (1957), was selected by NASA as the official astronaut's watch, a position it has retained. Being the first watch worn on the moon – not by Neil Armstrong, who left his watch in the lunar lander, but by Buzz Aldrin – has underpinned interest in Omega products ever since.

But the Speedmaster is not the only watch on which Omega's reputation has been built. The Seamaster line of watches, introduced in 1948 – Omega's longest-running series – was based around rugged watches designed for the Royal Navy during World War II. It borrowed a waterproof seal from submarine design and was the on-screen James

Bond's watch of choice from 1995. Meanwhile, the Constellation line, introduced in 1952, won a deserved reputation for accuracy.

Omega became Official Timekeeper of the Olympic Games 1932, introducing the brand to vast new audiences. This long-standing arrangement requires huge and constant investment in technology and equipment by the company. In 1948, for example, Omega developed the first cellular, photoelectric timing system, dubbed 'magic eye' to help record accurate finishing times, after it was discovered that previous models had been sensitive to flashes of sunlight. It marked the advent of electronic time-keeping at sports events.

PAGE 104: The Omega Speedmaster Collection.
OPPOSITE: Omega Constellation.

Constellation
CO-AXIAL

ABOVE: Poster advertising the Speedmaster as the first watch on the moon.

OMEGA SPEEDMASTER

Maker: Omega / *Watch:* Speedmaster / *Launched:* 1957

HISTORY

NASA tested chronographs from 10 brands anonymously purchased in Houston, Texas, in 1962, and Omega won the official NASA account three years later, actually with a version of a watch launched in 1957, ten months before *Sputnik*.

FUNCTIONALITY

The Speedmaster used acrylic glass that gave maximum visibility in all conditions, but would not shatter into hundreds of tiny pieces if broken. The watch was designed to operate in a vacuum and zero gravity. It could withstand temperature extremes on the moon of -160 to +120 degrees C, as well as the huge G-forces of take-off and re-entry.

IMPACT

On the Apollo 13 mission of 1972, a complete systems failure meant astronauts on board had to time the rocket burst that aligned their capsule for re-entry to the Earth's atmosphere using their Speedmasters. As one advertisement put it: "Tested in Switzerland. Tested in Houston. Tested on the Moon".

ROLEX

Rolex, unquestionably the biggest name in watchmaking, began life in 1905 as Wilsdorf & Davis, when the company was established in London by Hans Wilsdorf, a 24-year-old German. As much a great marketing mind as a watchmaker, Wilsdorf registered the company in La Chaux-de-Fonds as Rolex three years later, the name said to be inspired by the sound of winding a mechanical watch. The brand quickly won a reputation for precision, but it was Wilsdorf's drive to make a much more robust watch – resulting in the Oyster, the first dust- and waterproof watch, in 1926 – that truly set the company apart.

Rolex would go on to introduce many watchmaking innovations of a utilitarian bent: the first 360-degree automatic rotor (hence the 'perpetual' branding, because the watch is constantly being wound while worn); the first watch with a date display, the Datejust (1945); the first to display day and date, the Day-Date (1956); and the Milgauss (1956), first watch able to withstand magnetic fields of up to 1000 gauss. Rolex tested watches in extreme conditions, fixing prototypes of its Sea-Dweller (1967) to the side of submersibles, including the *Trieste* on its voyage 11,000 m (36,000 ft) down to the bottom of the Mariana Trench, the deepest point in the oceans.

ROLEX
OYSTER PERPETUAL
28

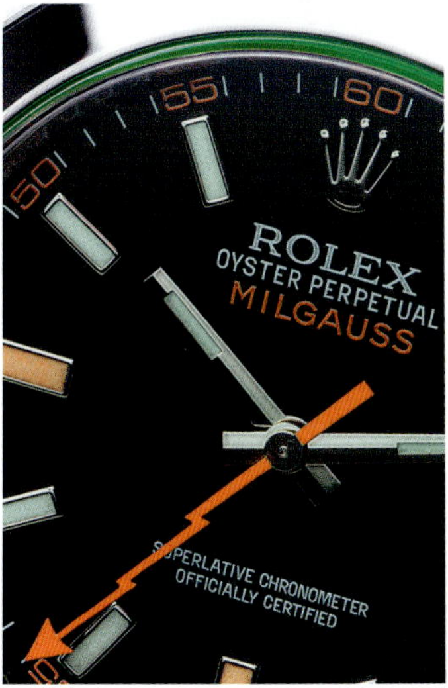
55
60
50
ROLEX
OYSTER PERPETUAL
MILGAUSS
OFFICIALLY CERTIFIED

UNITS PER HOUR
ROLEX
OYSTER PERPETUAL
SUPERLATIVE CHRONOMETER
OFFICIALLY CERTIFIED
COSMOGRAPH
DAYTONA
SWISS
MADE

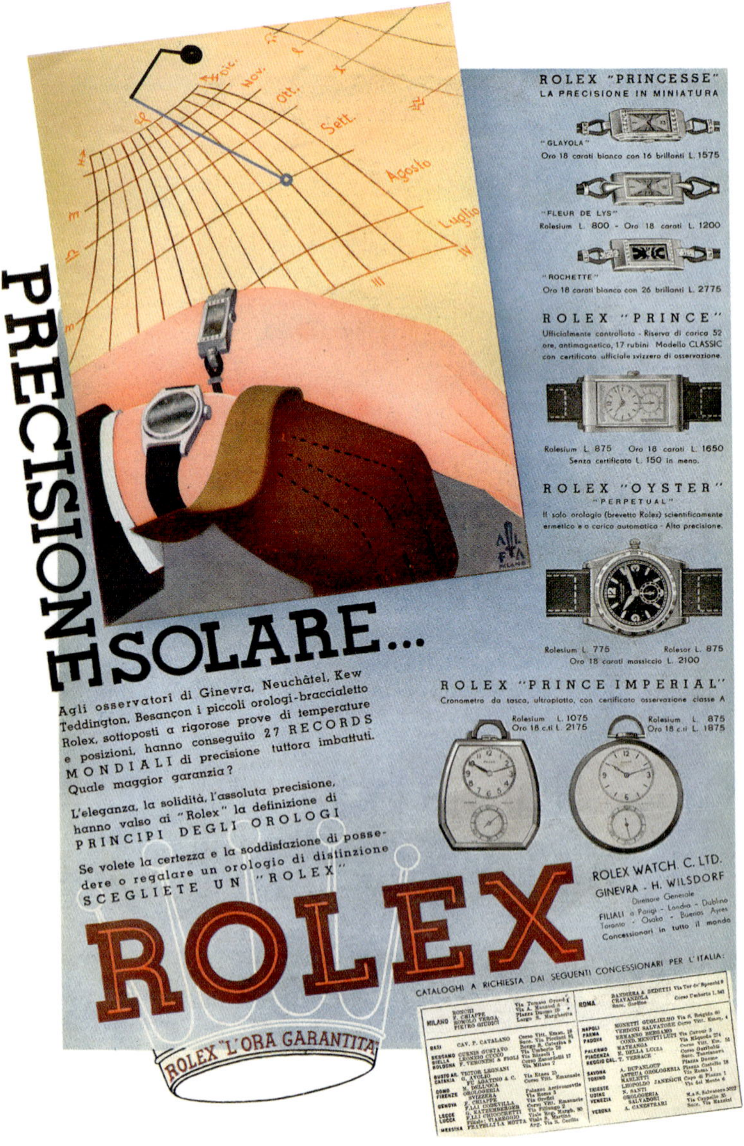

PRECISIONE SOLARE...
Agli osservatori di Ginevra, Neuchâtel, Kew Teddington, Besançon i piccoli orologi-braccialetto Rolex, sottoposti a rigorose prove di temperature e posizioni, hanno conseguito 27 RECORDS MONDIALI di precisione tuttora imbattuti. Quale maggior garanzia?
L'eleganza, la solidità, l'assoluta precisione, hanno valso ai "Rolex" la definizione di PRINCIPI DEGLI OROLOGI
Se volete la certezza e la soddisfazione di possedere o regalare un orologio di distinzione SCEGLIETE UN "ROLEX"
ROLEX
ROLEX "L'ORA GARANTITA"
ROLEX "PRINCESSE"
LA PRECISIONE IN MINIATURA
"GLAYOLA"
Oro 18 carati bianco con 16 brillanti L. 1575
"FLEUR DE LYS"
Rolesium L. 800 - Oro 18 carati L. 1200
"ROCHETTE"
Oro 18 carati bianco con 26 brillanti L. 2775
ROLEX "PRINCE"
Ufficialmente controllato - Riserva di carica 52 ore, antimagnetico, 17 rubini Modello CLASSIC con certificato ufficiale svizzero di osservazione.
Rolesium L. 875 Oro 18 carati L. 1650
Senza certificato L. 150 in meno.
ROLEX "OYSTER"
"PERPETUAL"
Il solo orologio (brevetto Rolex) scientificamente ermetico e a carica automatica - Alto precisione.
Rolesium L. 775 Rolesor L. 875
Oro 18 carati massiccio L. 2100
ROLEX "PRINCE IMPERIAL"
Cronometro da tasca, ultrapiatto, con certificato osservazione classe A
Rolesium L. 1075
Oro 18 c.ti L. 2175
Rolesium L. 875
Oro 18 c.ti L. 1875
ROLEX WATCH. C. LTD.
GINEVRA - H. WILSDORF
Direttore Generale
FILIALI a Parigi - Londra - Dublino
Toronto - Osaka - Buenos Ayres
Concessionari in tutto il mondo
CATALOGHI A RICHIESTA DAI SEGUENTI CONCESSIONARI PER L'ITALIA:

But these technical achievements were arguably superseded by the sheer number of enduring Rolex designs that came to be perceived not just as classics, but the definition of the form. The Submariner (1953), for example, remains the archetype of the diving watch and the Cosmograph Daytona (1963), among the rarest and most desirable collector's watches, is often perceived as the ultimate in chronographs. Even the company's bracelet designs, the Oyster and the Jubilee are recognizable.

PREVIOUS PAGE: (Top) Oyster Perpetual Datejust; (bottom left) Milgauss; (bottom right) Daytona.
OPPOSITE: Italian Rolex poster, 1939.
ABOVE: Datejust.

ABOVE: The Submariner has been endlessly copied by other brands.

ROLEX SUBMARINER

Maker: Rolex / *Watch:* Submariner / *Launched:* 1953

HISTORY

Rolex's Director of Communications, René-Paul Jeanneret, was a keen diver and first conceived of the Submariner at a time when diving was still a specialist activity. Testing involved creating a prototype watch, a Deep Sea Special, and taking it to depths of 3,150 m (10,335 ft) on the side of scientist and deep-sea explorer Jacques Piccard's bathyscaphe *Trieste*.

FUNCTIONALITY

It was the first watch to have what Rolex called a 'revolutionary time-recorder', better known today as the calibrated bezel, which could be turned and set with zero aligning with the minute hand in order to display elapsed time underwater. The winding crown was fitted with a 'Twinlock' gasket, which virtually guaranteed no water could get inside the movement.

IMPACT

Though not the first diving watch, the Submariner was the most influential. It was the watch of the Sean Connery-era James Bond.

CASIO

The Kashio brothers started a business in postwar Tokyo, making a steel pipe designed for hands-free smoking. It would be another decade before their business made a radical shift, with the launch in 1957 of an innovative portable calculator. That same year, the company adopted a new name: Casio Computer Co. This is the same Casio that created the F-91W LCD digital watch (1989), in terms of units sold, the most popular watch in history.

Casio had launched its first watch, the Casiotron QW01, in 1974 – essentially because too many other companies had started making calculators. It was swiftly followed by the QW02 (1974), the first digital perpetual calendar, and the X1 (1976), with a stopwatch and time-zone function.

Casio's mission was to pack its watches – often made of tough resin – with as much functionality as possible; 1980 saw the launch of the C-80, the first calculator watch that didn't require a stylus to operate it. Casio's greatest contribution to watchmaking was yet to come in the G-Shock. Collectible and often 'modded' to rival the Swatch, it became a cult, with models including the AE-1200 'Casio Royale' World Timer (2012) and the GA-2100-1A (2019), dubbed the 'CasiOak', after Audemar Piguet's Royal Oak.

ABOVE: The Casio alarm chrono W-59, a water-resistant version of the iconic F-91W.

ABOVE: This Casio G-Shock is a modern iteration of the hugely popular 5600 series, which originally debuted in the 1980s.

CASIO G-SHOCK

Maker: Casio / *Watch:* G-Shock / *Launched:* 1983

HISTORY

After 200 prototypes, engineer Kikuo Ibe created a watch that could literally be dropped from a height of 10 m (30 ft) and survive. In a TV advertisement, the company demonstrated this by using a G-Shock as an ice hockey puck.

FUNCTIONALITY

The G-Shock was water resistant to 100 m (300 ft) and had a 10-year battery life. To be so tough the first G-Shock, the DW-5000C, packed its digital module in a foam cradle, wrapped a rubber bumper and steel case around that, and put the whole lot in a resin shell.

IMPACT

The G-Shock overturned the idea that watches were delicate instruments, and set new benchmarks for watches used during sport, outdoor pursuits and in the military. It rivalled Swatch for collectability and artistic collaboration.

ABOVE: A poster for the Big Bang. This iteration combines ceramic, red gold and rubber.

HUBLOT

Hublot has always been somewhat controversial. Founded in 1976 by Italian watchmaker Carlo Crocco, it launched the MDM (1980), which had a porthole-style case (*hublot* is French for porthole) and a bezel laden with visible screws. What shocked at the time was that design combined a precious material – the gold case – with a black rubber strap. This bold and unexpected mixing of materials, the 'art of fusion' as the company described it, appealed to some, among them Giorgio Armani, King Juan Carlos of Spain and Elton John. But it confused many traditionalists, especially given Hublot's high prices.

When watch industry impresario Jean-Claude Biver took over the running of Hublot in 2004, he introduced what would become Hublot's Grand Prix d'Horlogerie de Géneve Design prize-wining icon, the similarly porthole-inspired Big Bang, which has since seen many iterations with unusual material combinations. The superlight Mag Bang (2007), for example, used an aluminium/magnesium alloy for case, bezel and movement. Others used tungsten, titanium, Kevlar, Hublot's proprietary scratch-resistant Magic Gold and, in the case of the Big Bang Sapphire (2016), crystal.

CITIZEN

Back in the 1970s, the revolutionary concept of a battery-powered, quartz-movement watch raised a problem: what to do with all the spent batteries. It was the Japanese company Citizen that started to work on a solution, its most promising idea being to place in a watch a photovoltaic cell that would convert light to energy. That notion had been explored before, with the mid-60s Synchronar 2100 LED. But no company had yet worked out a way of using a solar cell to power an analogue watch, until Citizen launched the Crystron Solar Cell (1976).

Founded as the Shokosha Watch Research Institute in 1918, 'Citizen' was first used as a name on a pocket watch in 1924 – promoting the brand's accessible pricing. It became the world leader in using light from any source for power. Where the Crystron could go for a week on a charge, by 1995 Citizen's watches, now with lithium-ion cells, could last for six months. This idea gave rise to Citizen's Eco-Drive technology, using a translucent dial placed directly over a silicon photocell, to power the movement below. Launched in 2016, it was the thinnest-ever, light-powered analogue watch, running for 10 months on a single charge; its Caliber 0100 movement of 2019 gave models an unprecedented accuracy of +/- one second per year.

TOP: Citizen Eco-Drive WR100.
BOTTOM: Models of the Eco-Drive light-powered series.

SWATCH

The launch of the Swatch watch in 1983 saved the Swiss watch industry, introducing countless people to the idea of wearing a watch as a fashion accessory (the name Swatch comes from a conflation of 'Second' and 'Watch'). 'Why not get two or three?' one advertisement suggested.

The brainchild of Nicolas Hayek, then president of the SMH Group (later the Swatch Group), the concept itself was the work of engineers Elmar Mock and Jacques Müller. The first Swatches launched in 1983, a collection of 12 designs, the classic being the understated black case, white dial model.

The Swatch was highly practical for the user: at just 18 g (0.64 oz) it was superlight, but it was also waterproof to 30 m (95 ft), shock resistant, and accurate thanks to a Quartz movement. It was also practical for the manufacturer: comprising just 51 parts, in a single-piece pastiche case, the production of a Swatch could be fully automated.

While maintaining its fun vision, Swatch expanded its remit to other styles, including the transparent JELLY FISH (1985), collaborations with artists, the Swatch IRONY with a metal case (1994) and the ultrathin SKIN (1997). There are even Swatch versions of the OMEGA Speedmaster (Moonswatch; 2022).

TOP: IRONY Valentine's Day Special (1996).
BOTTOM: Collaboration with Analia Baggiano.

ABOVE: Limited edition BR 01 Burning Skull.

BELL & ROSS

Swiss-made, French-based Bell & Ross was founded by Bruno Belamich and Carlos Rosillo in 1992. In 1998 its Hydromax won the world record for water resistance, in part down to a system that filled the case with transparent liquid. Soon the brand's modernist, function-forward watches won professional contracts with French military aviators, Spacelab missions and bomb disposal teams, while its old-meets-modernism Vintage 123 line (2002) expressed the company's distinctive graphic language.

The big, circle-in-a-square BR 01 (2005) that became Bell & Ross's most iconic design was clearly inspired by aircraft cockpit instrumentation, scaled down for the wrist. 'It's these square watches that give us visibility because they're so distinctive, Belamich has said. 'No question that, without it, it all would have been that much harder for us as a young brand.'

While the company went on to develop other models, including a collection inspired by World War 1 era pilots' watches, Bell & Ross parlayed the BR 01 into multiple, striking, often more avant-garde iterations, such as BR 01 Burning Skull (2009) and BR 01 Radar (2010), the latter using three red-toned, concentric rotating discs, instead of hands, to display the time.

URWERK

When trainee watchmaker Felix Baumgartner got together with art student Martin Frei in 1995, 'to make cool watches, the result was Geneva-based Urwerk.

Their first watch, the UR-101 (1998), unveiled what went on to become the company's wandering hour display. Six years later, the UR-103 (2003) set the style with its patented revolving satellite complication. Such watches required fresh thinking – the use of high-tech, superlight materials to compensate for the fact that the satellite complication weighs 160 times more than traditional hands, for example.

New ideas came with each model: the UR-202 Hammerhead (2008) was the first watch with a winding rate regulated by fluid dynamics and the CC1 King Cobra (2009) used two revolving cylinders to form a linear time display. The EMC Timehunter (2013) even came with an inbuilt device that measured the watch's accuracy and allowed the user to make their own adjustments. 'Watchmakers tend to think like watchmakers, doing what has been done before ... but engineers inevitably look to all sorts of ways to solve a problem,' Frei noted. 'Two hands on a watch is a rather limited way of expressing time, but with a linear display, for example, you get a rather different relationship with time.'

CLOCKWISE FROM TOP LEFT: Fulfilling Urwerk's ambition to make art that tells time – the UR-101, the UR-103, the UR-202 and the EMC.

RICHARD MILLE

Richard Mille, former President of the Watchmaking Division and Chief Executive Officer of the Jewellery Division, launched his eponymous Swiss watch company in 2001, along with business partner Dominique Guenat. His approach was deliberately disruptive and, for enthusiasts, a breath of fresh air. His vision was to maintain a signature style, a 'wraparound' tonneau case, and to apply the latest in materials and engineering to create aggressively contemporary, sports-oriented watches. The RM 056 (2012) was the first all-sapphire crystal, totally transparent watch.

Mille worked with tennis champion Rafael Nadal to develop the RM 27-01 (2013), a watch in which the entire movement is free-floating, suspended on four 0.35-mm-thick, braided steel cables. It is said to be able to withstand accelerations of over 5,000 G. Its case is made out of carbon nanotubes, meaning that the watch, including strap, weighs just 18,83 g (less than ¾ oz).

The company has also devised innovative novelties: the RM 11-01 Automatic Flyback Chronograph Roberto Mancini (2013) is designed for football matches. The dial displays match time based on each 45-minute half and can take up to 15 minutes stoppage time into account.

ABOVE: RM 27-04 Rafa Nadal, 2025.

ABOVE: The RM 001.

RICHARD MILLE RM001

Maker: Richard Mille / *Watch:* RM 001 / *Launched:* 2001

HISTORY

Richard Mille's first watch was a tourbillon, but that was the only way in which it was traditional. The brand set out to apply aerospace and Formula 1 technology to watchmaking.

FUNCTIONALITY

The RM 001 broke watchmaking 'rules' in having a very high production cost and yet made of industrial materials such as titanium, which made it one of the toughest and lightest tourbillons at the time. It had a power-reserve indicator, but also a torque indicator to prevent over-winding.

IMPACT

Aesthetically, the RM 001 introduced a disruptive modernity to watch design not just in terms of materials, but with its extremely complicated, curved tonneau watch case, visible screws, 3D-effect dial and unorthodox calibre, on show both front and back.

TOP: HM4 'Thunderbolt'.
BOTTOM: (Left) Legacy Machine No.1; (right) HM1.

MB&F

Before setting up his own independent watch company in 2005, Maximilian Büsser was managing director of Harry Winston Rare Timepieces. But it is for MB&F and its outlandish, cultish 'horological machines' that Büsser really made his mark in the industry. MB&F stands for Max Büsser & Friends – a nod to the many experts he collaborates with, among them watch designer Eric Giroud.

The watches take shape as time-telling, wearable sculptures, produced in limited numbers: HM3 'Frog' (2009), for example, and the futuristic HM4 'Thunderbolt' (2010). 'After all, [watches in this age] don't have to be practical, and if they're not practical they can be artistic, and if they are artistic, why bother chasing ideas of practicality?' Büsser has asked.

Nevertheless, MB&F might contest that its award-winning, avant-garde approach couples radical movement design with its futuristic exterior styling. This is evident in the debut HM1 (2007), which had the world's first four-mainspring barrel arrangement; and the pioneering 'flying' balance wheel and vertical power reserve indicator of the more classical Legacy Machine No.1 (2011). Other technical accomplishments include an error-proof perpetual calendar and the world's fastest triple-axis regulator.

RESSENCE

Benoît Mintiens would admit that he never thought about designing a watch until he visited a watch trade show one year, only to be amazed to see 'so many watches with such low levels of creativity'. So, in 2010 the Belgian industrial designer set about designing a watch himself.

Up to this point, Mintiens had been involved in the design of the Eurostar train and of the new-generation TGV train for SNCF. He'd designed first-class interiors for Air France, strollers for Maxi-Cosi and vacuum cleaners for LG Electronics. His Swiss-made Type 1, Type 2 and Type 3 watches not only introduced pioneering ideas, but recalibrated watch aesthetics. They are curvy, pebble-like pieces with single-layer dials extending out to the very edge of the watch to maximize surface area and make them easier to read. In one model, the space between dial and glass is oil-filled to prevent the refraction of light, so minimizing the human eye's depth perception, again making it easier to read. Ressence watches also have a lever set into the case-back rather than a traditional crown. Why so? Because, Mintiens would argue, to have the mechanism protruding from the device makes about as much sense as an engine winder would on a modern car.

ABOVE: (Top) TYPE 11 PINE; (centre left) TYPE 2 GREY: (bottom right): TYPE 3 EUCALYPTUS.

APPLE

While mechanical watches exemplify tradition, history, craft and innovation, it's undeniable that (much to the watch industry's consternation) wrists in the 21st century have been dominated by smartwatches – wrist-worn interfaces for smartphones – and by the Apple Watch in particular. Apple's was not the first smartwatch; as far back as 1983 Seiko was producing its Data 2000, a watch that could store data and synch with a PC, and later its Ruputer (1998), which ran apps. The same year saw computer engineering academic Steve Mann create the WearComp, the first smartwatch. Fossil/Palm, Microsoft and Sony Ericsson subsequently entered the fledgling smartwatch market, too.

Yet it was with the launch of the Apple Watch in 2015 that this market exploded, with its smartphone connectivity, OLED display and activity tracking in a curvaceous, Jony Ive–designed form. There have been many iterations, including one in 18-karat gold. Series 2 was water-resistant, Series 3 had cellular connectivity, and later versions were slimmer, lighter, faster and tougher, some even with a 100-m (300-ft) depth rating.

OPPOSITE: (Top left and right) Apple watches, Series 1; (Bottom) Apple allows its smartwatch to have an analogue dial.

Activity
10:09
MOVE
EXERCISE
STAND

<Jamie

PICTURE CREDITS

The publisher would like to thank the following individuals and organizations for their kind permission to reproduce the images in this book. Every effort has been made to acknowledge the pictures, however, we apologize if there are any unintentional omissions.

t: top, b: bottom, l: left, r: right

Cover: Shutterstock/saeid poorat

Alamy: 14tr adsR, 17 f8 archive, 28 Prisma by Dukas Presseagentur GmbH, 31 adsR, 37t Retro AdArchives, 52 adsR, 55b Valery Voennyy, 61 adsR, 85bl Grzegorz Czapski, 89 adsR, 103b Tubray Media, 108 adsR, 118 Hugh Threlfall, 120 adsrR, 125t adsR, 125bl adsR, 125br, 139tl Grzegorz Czapski, 139tr Grzegorz Czapski

AnOrdain: 85t

Breguet: 73

Getty: 7 John Sciulli, 8b Bloomberg, 10 TPLP, 13 Kirn Vintage Stock, 14tl swim ink 2 llc, 14b Bob Olsen, 21 Bloomberg, 22b ozgurdonmaz, 26 Frederic REGLAIN, 34t Bloomberg, 37bl Anwar Hussein, 37br Sunset Boulevard, 39 TV Times, 39 inset TIMOTHY A. CLARY, 51 MICHAEL BUHOLZER, 55t Science & Society Picture Library, 55m Science & Society Picture Library, 71 Robb Report, 74t Matthew Peyton, 85br Bloomberg, 86 JUSTIN TALLIS, 92b Craig Barritt, 97 Eugene Gologursky, 100 Robb Report, 106 Bloomberg, 112 Fireshot, 123b Bloomberg, 126 RICHARD JUILLIART

IWC: 91t, 91b

Lange Uhren GmbH: 80t, 80bl, 80br

MB&F: 134

Ming: 40t

Ressence: 137t, 137m, 137b

Richard Mille: 132

Shutterstock: 3 saeid poorat, 8t Nordroden, 22t PHLD Luca, 33 CapturePB, 45 imickle82, 46t SimoneN, 46b Rudenkois, 58t Maulana Noriandita, 58b Felix Schier, 65 Robert Way, 68 PingPong56, 74b jeafish Ping, 77 i viewfinder, 92t Matthew Bain Inc, 94 Zuumy, 103t Travelwith Nikon, 104 Thomas Bang Petersen, 111t LEVANTEMEDIA, 111bl keyvisuals, 111br VGI, 113b Kim Diaz, 117 Zuyeu Uladzimir, 123t DW labs Incorporated, 131 Zuumy

Studio Underd0g: 40bl, 40br

Ulysse Nardin: 67, 83

Unsplash: 114 Patrick Langwallner, 125, 139

Urwerk: 34b, 42, 129

AUTHOR ACKNOWLEDGEMENTS

With thanks to the world's watchmakers for keeping their functional art alive against the odds. And to Pelham and Renwick for teaching the true importance of time.

OTHER BOOKS AVAILABLE

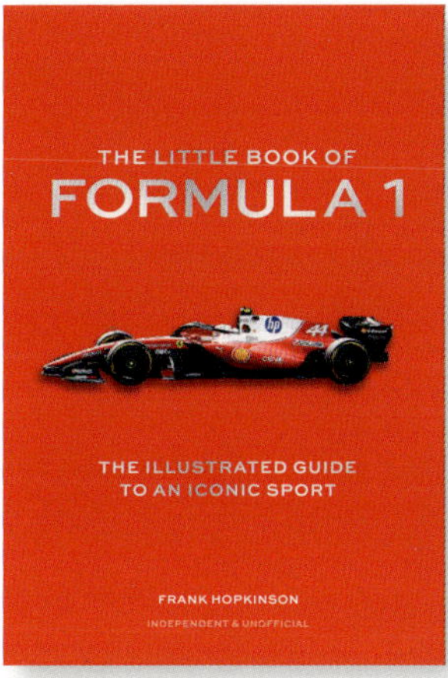

ISBN: 978-1-78840-699-4

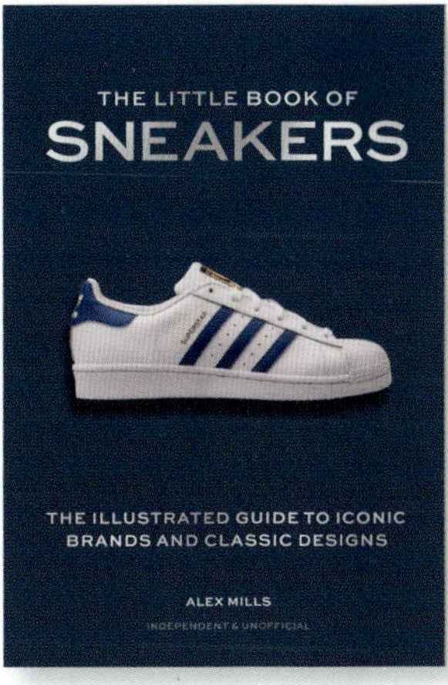

ISBN: 978-1-78840-697-0

RAISING READERS
Books Build Bright Futures

Dear Reader,

We'd love your attention for one more page to tell you about the crisis in children's reading, and what we can all do.

Studies have shown that reading for fun is the **single biggest predictor of a child's future life chances** – more than family circumstance, parents' educational background or income. It improves academic results, mental health, wealth, communication skills, ambition and happiness.[1]

The number of children reading for fun is in rapid decline. Young people have a lot of competition for their time. In 2024, 1 in 10 children and young people in the UK aged 5 to 18 did not own a single book at home.[2]

Hachette works extensively with schools, libraries and literacy charities, but here are some ways we can all raise more readers:

- Reading to children for just 10 minutes a day makes a difference
- Don't give up if children aren't regular readers – there will be books for them!
- Visit bookshops and libraries to get recommendations
- Encourage them to listen to audiobooks
- Support school libraries
- Give books as gifts

There's a lot more information about how to encourage children to read on our website: **www.RaisingReaders.co.uk**

Thank you for reading.

hachette LIVRE

[1] OECD, '21st-Century Readers: Developing Literacy Skills in a Digital World', 2021, https://www.oecd.org/en/publications/21st-century-readers_a83d84cb-en.html

[2] National Literacy Trust, 'Book Ownership in 2024'. November 2024, https://literacytrust.org.uk/research-services/research-reports/book-ownership-in-2024